I'M WALKING WITH JESUS DAY BY DAY
STEPS
FOR MY JOURNEY

I'm Walking With Jesus Day By Day
STEPS
FOR MY JOURNEY

NANCY JO SWAN

Copyright © 2023 Nancy Jo Swan

Cover Design: Soleil Branding Essentials
Internal Layout: Angelique A. Strothers of 963 Publishing
Author Photo and Internal Photo Editor: Aaron D. Jones of AJ97media
Editor: Theresa A. Edwards

ISBN Number (Hardcover) 978-1-7357407-4-4

Volume One

Unless otherwise indicated, all Scripture quotations are from the ESV® Bible (The Holy Bible English Standard Version®), copyright © 2001 by Crossway, a publishing ministry of Good News Publishers. Used by permission. All rights reserved.

Scripture quotations marked (NLT) are taken from the *Holy Bible,* New Living Translation, copyright © 1996, 2004, 2015 by Tyndale House Foundation. Used by permission of Tyndale House Publishers, Carol Stream, Illinois 60188. All rights reserved.

Scripture quotations marked CSB have been taken from the Christian Standard Bible ®, Copyright © 2017 by Holman Bible Publishers. Used by permission. Christian Standard Bible® and CSB® are federally registered trademarks of Holman Publishers.

Scripture taken from the New King James Version®. Copyright © 1982 by Thomas Nelson. Used by permission. All rights reserved.

Scripture quotations marked (NIV) are taken from the Holy Bible, New International Version®, NIV®. Copyright © 1973, 1978, 1984, 2011 by Biblica, Inc. ™ Used by permission of Zondervan. All rights reserved worldwide. www.zondervan.com The "NIV" and "New International Version" are trademarks registered in the United States Patent and Trademark Office by Biblica, Inc. ™

This book is presented to:

_____St Regis_____

Given with love by:

_____Kathy Samek_____

On this date:

_____April 2024_____

Occasion:

_____For the children to learn about Jesus_____

"I have no greater joy than to hear that my children are walking in truth."
3 John 1:4

In Loving Memory Of

My Precious Granddaughter, Kamryn Lachelle-Rose Swan
June 8, 2005 – November 10, 2020

Dedicated to

Caleb Joseph Baza, my adorable great-grandson

"I praise you, for I am fearfully and wonderfully made..."
Psalm 139:14a

Giving Thanks

Thank you, my Lord, for your Amazing Grace, and your love like no other towards me.

"Commit your work to the Lord, and your plans will be established."
Proverbs 16:3

Thank you for your friendship and love:
William "Billy" Good
Shan & Darrell Felder
Theresa A. Edwards
Aaron D. Jones
Angelique A. Strothers

Thank You, God, for my mom, my family, extended family and my village, who have walked with me step by step... God bless each of you, abundantly!

"A friend loves at all times..."
Proverbs 17:17

To the Parents and Village: A Note About the Book

I am so excited that you are walking with your children day by day as they embrace their personal relationship with Jesus. _I'm Walking with Jesus, Day by Day_ Devotional/Journal consists of 52 weeks of scriptures, one scripture a week to memorize, hide in their hearts and journal as they go. Please allow your children to express their personal walk as they journal or draw on each page. Allow them to be creative and excited along the way; however, take as long as your children need to embrace the scripture. While _I'm Walking with Jesus Day by Day_ is recommended for children ages five and up who are reading and writing, it can also be introduced to toddlers or even while a child is still in his mother's womb. The purpose of the book is for children to encounter God through scripture, meditation, and journaling as they walk day by day with Jesus. Hopefully, while journeying and journaling, children will learn the importance of tucking the word of God in their hearts, memorizing scripture, and applying it to their daily lives.

*All scriptures are English Standard Version unless otherwise noted.

"For you formed my inward parts you knitted me together in my mother's womb." – Psalm 139:13
"I have stored up your word in my heart that I might not sin against you." Psalm 119:11 NIV

Suggested Steps

In *Walking with Jesus Day by Day*, memorizing scripture is an important step towards a child understanding scripture. After reading a specific verse, parents should ask the child what the scripture means to him. Then point out words throughout the scripture verse and ask the child for explanations. Once the child offers his interpretation emphasize unfamiliar words and explain their meanings to assist in the child's comprehension. Remember that each scripture verse must be read repeatedly for memorization, and that memorization of a given verse may take longer than a week. Introducing different Bible translations is another exciting method of studying the scripture verse. Following are examples of focusing on words in verses:

Example 1:
Psalm 119:11 *NLT*
I have hidden your word in my heart,
That I might not sin against you.

Words to Point Out might be:
Hidden
Your
Word
Heart
Not Sin
A suggested question might be, "Sin against whom?"

Example 2: *Different Version*
Psalm 119:11 *CSB*
I have treasured your word in my heart so that I may not sin against you.

Word to Point Out
Treasured

*Introducing new translations will typically be used after children are comfortable with the initial translation used. Children enjoy learning new words, which can create a nice family time of sharing and learningSAMPLE

What does "blessed" mean?

July 7th, 2023

I want to believe God too... God, can you help me believe?

July 12th, 2023

Luke 1:45

"You are blessed because you believed that the Lord would do what He said."

Hmm....... What does God say about me?

July 23rd, 2023

SAMPLE PAGE

Week 1

Psalm 139:13

"For you formed my inward parts;
you knitted me together in my mother's womb."

Week 1

Week 2

Psalm 139:14a

"I praise you, for I am fearfully and wonderfully made."

Week 2

Week 3

Colossians 3:16a

"Let the word of Christ dwell in you richly..."

Week 4

Numbers 6: 24-26

"The Lord bless you and keep you; the Lord make his face to shine upon you and be gracious to you; the Lord lift up His countenance upon you and give you peace."

Week 4

Genesis 1:1

"In the beginning God created the heavens and the earth."

Week 5

STEP BY STEP

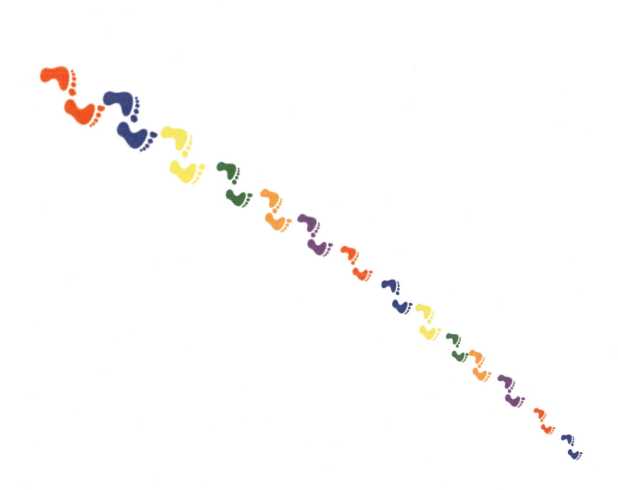

STEP BY STEP

Week 6

Proverbs 16:3

"Commit your work to the Lord,
and your plans will be established."

Week 6

Psalm 23: 1-6

"The Lord is my shepherd; I shall not want,
He makes me lie down in green pastures,
He leads me beside still waters.
He restores my soul.
He leads me in paths of righteousness for his name's sake.
Even though I walk through the valley of the shadow of death,
I will fear no evil, for you are with me;
Your rod and your staff, they comfort me.
You prepare a table before me in the presence of my enemies;
You anoint my head with oil; my cup overflows.
Surely goodness and mercy shall follow me all the days of my life,
And I shall dwell in the house of the Lord forever."

Week 8

Colossians 3:20

"Children, obey your parents in everything, for this pleases the Lord."

Week 8

Philippians 4:13

"I can do all things through him who strengthens me."

Week 10

Psalm 150:6

"Let everything that has breath praise the Lord!
Praise the LORD!"

Week 10

Jeremiah 29:11

"For I know the plans I have for you, declares the Lord, plans for welfare and not for evil, to give you a future and a hope"

Week 12

Matthew 5:14a

"You are the light of the world…"

Week 12

Psalm 145:9

"The Lord is good to all,
and his mercy is over all that he has made."

MY JOURNEY

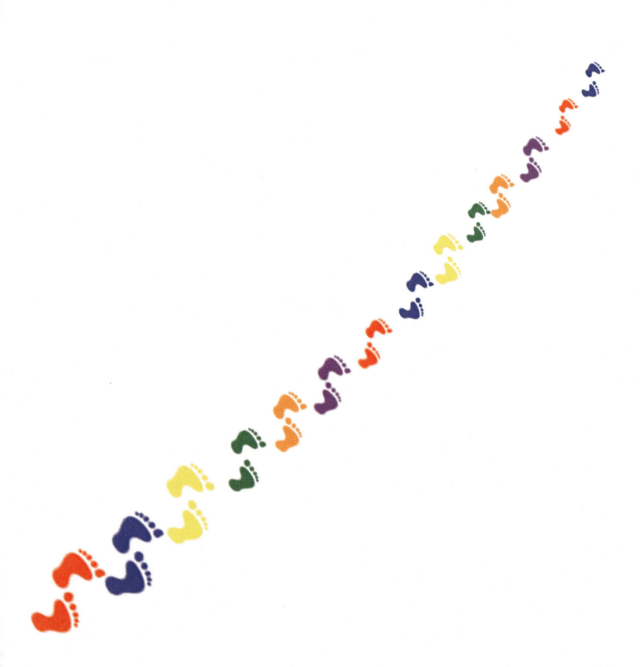

MY JOURNEY

Week 14

James 1:17a

"Every good gift and every perfect gift is from above..."

Week 14

Matthew 28:20b

"…I am with you always! …"

~Miss Nancy

Matthew 6:9-13 (NKJV)

"In this manner, therefore, pray:
Our Father in heaven,
Hallowed be Your name.
Your kingdom come.
Your will be done
On earth as it is in heaven.
Give us this day our daily bread.
And forgive us our debts,
As we forgive our debtors.
And do not lead us into temptation,
But deliver us from the evil one.
For Yours is the kingdom and the power and the glory forever.
Amen."

Week 17

Romans 3:23

"For all have sinned and fall short of the glory of God."

Week 17

Week 18

Romans 10:13

"For 'everyone who calls on the name of the Lord will be saved.'"

Acts 16:31

"...Believe in the Lord Jesus, and you will be saved..."

Believe child!!
~Miss Nancy

Week 20

Ephesians 6:1

"Children, obey your parents in the Lord, for this is right."

Ephesians 4:32a

"Be kind to one another…"

Kamryn would always say, "Kindness is everything, Granny."
~ Miss Nancy

Week 22

1 John 3:23

"And this is his commandment, that we believe in the name of his Son Jesus Christ and love one another, just as he has commanded us."

Week 23

Psalm 119:105

"Your word is a lamp to my feet and a light to my path."

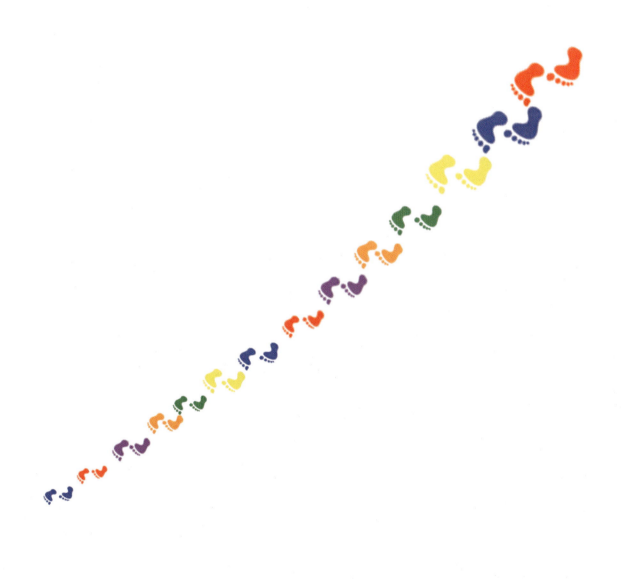

Week 23

Week 24

Proverbs 3:5-6

"Trust in the Lord with all your heart,
and do not lean on your own understanding.
In all your ways acknowledge him,
and he will make straight your paths."

Week 24

Hebrews 13:8 (NLT)

"Jesus Christ is the same yesterday, today and forever."

Week 26

Isaiah 43:5a (NLT)

"Do not be afraid for I am with you."

Week 26

Week 27

Matthew 28:6a

"He is not here, for he has risen[!]"

Week 27

Week 28

Psalm 136:1

"Give thanks to the LORD, for he is good,
for his steadfast love endures forever."

Week 28

Week 29

Luke 6:31

"And as you wish that others would do to you, do so to them."

Week 29

Week 30

John 10:11

"I am the good Shepherd.
The good shepherd lays down his life for the sheep."
Week 30

Week 31

Proverbs 30:5

**"Every word of God proves true;
he is a shield to those who take refuge in him."**

Matthew 19:13-14

"Then children were brought to him that he might lay his hands on them and pray. The disciples rebuked the people, but Jesus said, 'Let the little children come to me and do not hinder them, for to such belongs the kingdom of heaven.'"

Week 33

Psalm 27:1

"The LORD is my light and my salvation; whom shall I fear? The LORD is the stronghold of my life; of whom shall I be afraid?"

Week 34

Psalm 19:1

"The heavens declare the glory of God, and the sky above proclaims his handiwork."

Week 34

Proverbs 14:5

"A faithful witness does not lie,
but a false witness breathes out lies."

DAY BY DAY

DAY BY DAY

Week 36

Psalm 138:1 (NIV)

"I will praise you, LORD, with all my heart; before the "gods" I will sing your praise."

1 John 5:3

"For this is the love of God, that we keep his commandments. And his commandments are not burdensome."

Lamentations 3:22-24

"The steadfast love of the LORD never ceases; his mercies never come to an end; they are new every morning; great is your faithfulness. 'The LORD is my portion' says my soul, 'therefore I will hope in him.'"

Lamentations 3: 25-26

"The LORD is good to those who wait for him,
to the soul who seeks him.
It is good that one should wait quietly
for the salvation of the Lord."

Week 40

Lamentations 3:27 (NIV)

"It is good for a man to bear the yoke while he is young."

Galatians 6:7

"Do not be deceived; God is not mocked, for whatever one sows, that will he also reap."

Week 42

Matthew 22:39

"...you shall love your neighbor as yourself."

Week 42

1 Corinthians 10:31

"...whatever you do, do all to the glory of God."

Week 44

Deuteronomy 6:5

"You shall love the LORD your God with all your heart and with all your soul and with all your might."

Week 44

Week 45

Psalm 118:24

"This is the day that the LORD has made;
let us rejoice and be glad in it."

Week 46

Psalm 46:10a

"Be still, and know that I am God..."

Week 46

1 Thessalonians 5:17

"Pray without ceasing."

"Continue to pray even if your prayer is not answered the first time you pray!" ~Miss Nancy

Week 48

Proverbs 2:6

"For the LORD gives wisdom; from his mouth come knowledge and understanding."

Week 48

Week 49

Colossians 3:2

"Set your minds on things that are above,
not on things that are on earth."

Psalm 119:11

"I have hidden your word in my heart that I might not sin against you."

"To hide God's Word in your heart means to memorize and meditate on the Word of God." ~ Miss Nancy

Ecclesiastes 12:13b

"...Fear God and keep his commandments..."

Week 51

Ecclesiastes 3:1
"For everything there is a season, and a time for every matter under heaven."

Week 51

Week 52

Ecclesiastes 3:2

"A time to be born, and a time to die; a time to plant, and a time to pluck up what is planted."

"Always remember there is a time for everything."
~Miss Nancy

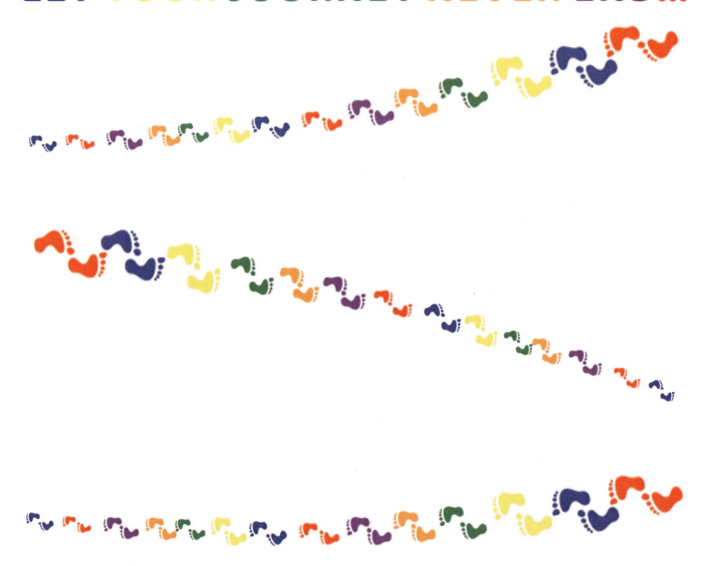

LET YOUR JOURNEY NEVER END...

KEEP WALKING WITH JESUS

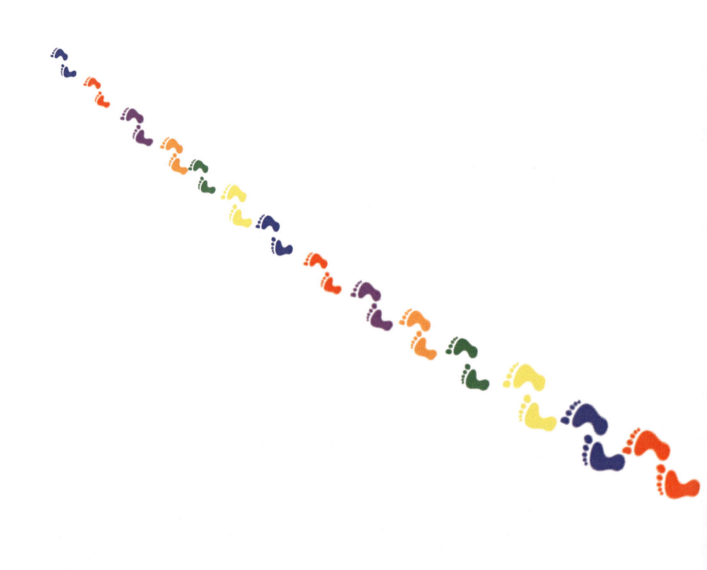

Nancy Jo Swan is the author of *I'm Walking with Jesus Day by Day: Steps for My Journey*. Nancy is retired from a successful career with Delta Airlines. Her love for children led her to serve for several years as Coordinator of Children's Ministries at Macedonia Church of Pittsburgh.

"Train up a child in the way he should go; even when he is old he will not depart from it..." ~ Prov. 22:6

Proverbs 22:6 was the basis for her teachings of Jesus for children ages one to twelve. Over the years, the young people she taught and mentored developed a great deal of admiration and respect for the woman they came to know as "Miss Nancy." Nancy believes Jesus Christ is the only way, on our daily journey.

Nancy is the great-grandmother of Caleb, grandmother of Mallory, Mackenzie and the late Kamryn and the mother of Kimberly and the late Wendy.

Made in the USA
Monee, IL
11 December 2023

27c91c1e-0c16-442c-abe7-25b1f4a73d9aR01